THE LAST ACHIEVEMENT

The Last Achievement

Willem Berger

A Grail Publication
1974

Originally published in Dutch
under the title *Pastorale begeleiding*

©Uitgeverij Ambo b.v.
First published in Holland 1973
First published in England 1974

©The Grail England
Translated by M. Ederveen

ISBN 0 901829 2 42

published by the Grail, 125 Waxwell Lane,
Pinner, Middlesex HA5 3ER

distribution: Grail Centre, 1066 London Road, Alvaston,
Derby DE2 8QA

Printed by Burleigh Ltd, The Burleigh Press, Bristol 1, England.

To Gerrit Pieter Bakker, my first parish priest,
in gratitude and friendship

CONTENTS

Contents

Preface

Recently I came across this quotation from the German poet, Rainer Maria Rilke: 'The wish to die one's own death is gradually becoming more exceptional. Before long this wish will be as rare as the wish to lead one's own life.' These words make a bitter judgement on the way we live and work together.

All the same, much of what I have read, and my own personal experience suggest that many people, when illness threatens their lives, do wish to come to terms with their own death and to die it. Yet at that very moment those around them organise a conspiracy of silence which makes this desire impossible to realise.

This booklet is written for people who do not want to isolate the ones they love and who are ready to try to break through this conspiracy of silence surrounding death. It is also meant for those who, when their own time of serious illness arrives, do not want to resign themselves to isolation from their surroundings, by a wall of lies and silence. In other words, it is meant for those who do want to die their own death and who realise that to some extent they need the help of those around them.

Finally this booklet is meant for the 'professionals'—doctors, clinical psychologists, ministers of the different churches and traditions. In the hour of death their primary task lies in re-establishing communion, in building bridges and especially in restoring communication about 'the state of being ultimately concerned.'

After long years of silence people in the Netherlands are beginning to say that it might be a liberating thing if in the face of death we knew how to speak, if need be, of God.

WILLEM BERGER

Nijmegen
June 1974

1
Counselling the dying: primarily the layman's task

A DYING man who is able to look back at the past with serenity and gratitude: this is the man whose last year of life is described in Rya Luysterburg's book *Death has all the time in the world*.[1] As the book begins the sick man has just learned from his doctor that his illness has been diagnosed as incurable. His daughter hears this from the doctor and goes to visit her father. She attempts to steer the conversation away from this difficult subject but without success. After this failure she tries to introduce a flippant note into the discussion of his illness. She fails again. From now onwards it is the sick father who directs the conversation. What he wants is to talk about his approaching death, to say goodbye to his family and his friends, to put his affairs in order. And more than anything else, he wants to express what life and death mean to him, to give witness to what he believes. The father exemplifies a modern way of believing, full of doubts, critical, yet in the last analysis tolerant and realistic.

At the beginning of his illness the man's wife is depicted with an element of caricature, as a self-centred and timorous believer. In her behaviour we see all the deficiencies that result when faith is used as self-defence or as a substitute for the security afforded by a protective group. These shortcomings are intrinsic to her character, but she has one saving grace: she is not so inflexible that she is incapable of change. For months she has been irritated and full of complaints, arguing that her husband would be far better off in a hospital or nursing home. She quails under the burden she has to bear and what she fears above all is to be faced with his dying. But as time passes, she is able to outgrow her old self and in the end she can cope with everything.

The daughter, the narrator in the story, has more affection

1

for her father than for her mother. She scarcely knows how to cope with his robust directness or with the depth of his feelings. But during that year of illness she changes too. She grows less fearful, more free. After her father has died the undertaker comes to remove the body. She says: "I've always thought this would be a terrible moment but it isn't any more. It's not my father who's being taken away. He is close to me, and we are at peace, we are happy."

Her father's last year was not just a year like any other. It was the last phase of his life and during these months a number of essential things had happened. Husband, wife and daughter had grown closer, barriers to communication had fallen, they had lost much of their fear, they had grown more courageous. When they said goodbye they felt that they had grown closer, that they would remain close. This process of deepening intimacy had been encouraged by the way the father had expressed his outlook on life and his convictions about life and death. He would have no pretence, he looked realistically at his friends, at his wife and her future, at himself. At a given moment a priest had come to assist the father. He was made welcome but he remained an outsider. He had no share in the intimacy of this family which was going through so much. He did his work satisfactorily, nothing more was expected of him. He came and he went away.

Every day deaths occur which do not result in the family growing closer.[2] This can be illustrated by the story of a widow aged sixty-two who had two daughters still living with her. She had cancer and radiation treatment had been stopped. The daughters knew that her prospects were very poor. The doctor suspected that his patient had some idea of the nature of her illness and he wanted to give her the opportunity of speaking with a priest. He asked her if the priest ever came to see her. This seemed not to be the case. The sick woman was grateful for the doctor's offer to invite one of the parish clergy to visit her. Throughout all this conversation one of the daughters had been present and as the doctor was leaving the house she implored him not to let the priest upset her mother when he came. In actual fact, it appeared that both daughters were terrified that they would not be able to cope with the resulting situation. The doctor telephoned the priest and both agreed that the patient needed to talk about her illness. However when the priest arrived he was given no chance to speak privately to the mother; the daughters remained present, listening to every word. During the next five weeks the priest came to the house only once. Later he appeared to give her the sacraments and after that he visited the sick woman every day. On the fifth day she died. Before her death the doctor praised her because she had borne her suffering with such fortitude and courage. But after her death he felt that her daughters had never expected their mother to show such bravery and were surprised by it. They admitted that she had faced the prospect of death much better than they had expected and feared, but they themselves had never been able to talk about death with her.

In the situation described by Rya Luysterburg it was the sick father who did the pastoral work, he who deepened the relationships within the family. The priest who came to administer the sacraments did not enter this family circle. He remained the *heilige aussenseiter* (the holy outsider).[3] Perhaps he had the opportunity and the task to encourage and deepen the family's growth in intimacy, still, this did not happen. In the other family the priest remained outside because the family shut him out. He met three people who did not dare to approach the subject of death. The daughters were terrified that the priest might introduce it because they had no idea how to cope. They kept him at arm's length and he, unassuming, respecting their fears and resistance, allowed them to do so. He could have helped them to re-establish relationships but he let the opportunity go by.

When a family is faced with illness and impending death this crisis has a double aspect. There is the aspect of danger, from which everyone tries to escape; there is the aspect of opportunity, the opportunity to discover a new and healthier pattern of life. The first aim of pastoral care is to help people to grasp this opportunity. It is not in the first place a task for 'professionals'. It is primarily something to be done within the community, the smaller and the larger community, to which each of us belongs. Professionals are there to help the sick person and those who surround him to give each other all they can give and wish to give, in particular to share their feelings about life and death. The job of the professional is often simply to remove the obstacles to this exchange. I say 'often' for although we have attacked the taboo around the subject of death, still this does not mean that we have learned to speak about the experience of impending death. The following example illustrates this.

A member of a group of theological students was suddenly taken seriously ill. He was rushed into hospital where an operation saved his life. On returning to the group he wanted to talk about his experiences. This was easier said than done. When he had suddenly found himself in a hospital bed the thought had come to him in a flash: None of my plans for next week are possible now because next week I'll still be here . . . or perhaps I shall be dead. This was what he wanted to tell his colleagues but he was given no opportunity. They didn't seem to want to hear it. They asked him all kinds of questions quite unrelated to his real story. He was at a loss for words, he looked around help-lessly. The one thing he wanted to do was to talk about his experiences, about the existential fears which had threatened him. He was unable to find the right words because nobody was listening to him. In the end the leader of the group asked the students if they realised what they were doing: Did they have some sort of objection to listening? It was only after further meetings that the young man could really discuss his story with the group.

There are various ways of describing this behaviour: flight, 'covering-up', escape. 'Covering-up' is also a signi-ficant word to describe one way of dealing with people who are close to death. An example of this concerns a young nurse on night duty who was looking after a middle-aged patient who was unquestionably dying. He badly wanted to talk, to give vent to something of his fears and hopes. But she gave him no opportunity. She was gentle, she was kind and attentive and she 'covered him up' very well. Today, years later, she recalls this with a certain bitterness, for she cannot forget what she did. She is not filled with remorse: she is level-headed enough to realise that she had never learned to do anything else.

The father in Rya Luysterburg's book will not let himself be 'covered-up'. The daughters of the dying widow will allow nothing else but 'covering-up'. The young nurse doesn't know what else she can do. The theological students get the opportunity to learn something about 'covering-up' and pastoral care through their group experience. One could say: I become a pastoral counsellor to my fellow-man if I give him the opportunity to reveal his deepest experiences, and do not try to cover them up.

The following example shows the necessity of taking action to restore communication within a family so that mutual pastoral care becomes possible. A man telephoned to tell me that his wife was seriously ill. I knew them both and he told me how he would appreciate it if I could visit her. She had been given the last sacraments a few days earlier but had scarcely realised it. She was very much confused and now appeared to be on the verge of death.

When I visited her I found this fifty-three year old woman surrounded by husband and children. She was regarding them with suspicion and anger. She said things which I couldn't immediately make sense of, yet in between she was entirely lucid. When I failed to react immediately to her confused remarks about her physical condition she regarded me with the same hostile suspicion. It is well known that dying people are quite capable of looking critically at themselves and their surroundings in spite of the fact that their powers of observation may sometimes be affected by illness. It is in the interests of everyone to go on appealing to this critical faculty as long as possible.[4] The sick person feels calmed and comforted if both he and the people around him can see that 'he is a bit confused but he shouldn't worry too much about it'. But in the case of this woman, my appeal to her own awareness of her confusion was in vain. Her husband asked if she would care to speak privately to me and she agreed. He and the children then withdrew. For another quarter of an hour I attempted to talk with her. It was a failure. She still remained hostile and suspicious and we both felt the pain of being unable to reach and make contact with the other. Then I asked if I could pray with her. She agreed and we said the Lord's Prayer together. After this I began to improvise. On her behalf I asked for gratitude for her life which in truth had been both good and successful. I asked for clarity of mind so that she could look death in the face— for the restoration of her old relationships with her husband and children and for a faithful surrender to God. Then I said the Hail Mary and she joined in up to the words 'pray for us sinners now and at the hour of our death'. At this point she looked hard at me and said: 'I know I'm confused but I can't stand it that everyone treats me like an idiot.' It then transpired that three years ago the doctor had told her husband that she was incurably ill. He had taken the doctor's advice to keep this knowledge from her as long as possible. When her illness became very grave he said nothing and when she was actually dying he was still silent, hoping to keep the secret until after her death.

One may ask why the woman didn't protest against this silence earlier, before she became confused. Weismann suggests that such a thing frequently happens. He describes a patient who also kept her anxieties to herself because she felt that both husband and doctor expected her to deceive herself as to the gravity of her illness. Moreover their expectation coincided only too well with her own reluctance to face the facts.[5] In the case of my friend's wife, her ability to join in this game of pretence[6] ceased as her self-control was broken down. The happy outcome of my intervention was a re-uniting of the whole family, and in this restored intimacy the woman lived for another four months no longer confused, but entirely lucid.

To summarise—pastoral help for the dying is first and foremost a task for the actual church community to which the person belongs. If those who stand around the dying person re-establish communion with him then he will be able to give them help as well as to receive help from them. Professional pastoral work is simply this: helping these people to help one another.

The next question is whether we can help each other in this way as a church community and what is meant by the 'consolations of the Church'.

2

What are 'the consolations of the Church'?

NOWADAYS the majority of people do not die at home but in a hospital or nursing home. Klink even says: 'Today it is becoming almost impossible to die at home.'[1] And when in fact a man is nursed by his family the demands of the situation often make him feel ill at ease with them and a burden. Yet this is the very time he needs his family and friends so much.

We can use different means to reach the patient, ways that teach us to feel how he is feeling and what his needs are. At a symposium held in Nijmegen in April 1973 called 'Dying with Human Dignity', J. Borst described how she had taught herself to feel how dependent you become on your fellow men when you are flat on your back and can hardly move at all.

Klink points out that the dying patient acquires a new status, a new rôle. He sets out on a final, clearly-defined phase in his career. It begins at the moment he knows that his illness will end in death or in a totally unexpected recovery. Each new role in life brings its own problems: a new job, marriage, the completion of divorce procedures, a second marriage, becoming unemployed or retired, being widowed. One has to learn to live in such a situation, and this is seldom achieved without stumbling. It always means learning to live in a way not known previously. Anyone who acquires the status of a dying person will have to get used to things that are completely new to him and to the fact that his body is altering, is increasingly becoming a burden. He will discover that his position among his friends and acquaintances has changed, (this is precisely what constitutes his new status), that he is now valued in a different way. Moreover he will be aware of different feelings and different experiences within himself. He will have to assimilate things he never expected to meet. He will certainly want to be able to express what his life and his death mean to him. This is why he needs help.

He needs help to sort out his feelings, to cope with his new relationship with his surroundings, and to give meaning to life and death. So he needs psychological and pastoral help. He particularly needs this support lest he should lose his bearings and his identity beneath the overwhelming mass of new impressions that pour over him. To put this into the language of faith: here is a situation in which a human being should be helped to realise that he has been created and redeemed and need not be lost. All the central themes of faith are relevant here—creation, the fall, the good news of redemption.

What does all this mean? I think we can understand without too much difficulty what it means to be no longer primarily a teacher, a housewife, an engineer or a bishop in the eyes of those around us, but somebody who is going to die. We can also grasp how hard it must be to learn to live with the signals being sent out by our bodies which remind us that we will never be our old selves again. The sadness, the fear and the despair are all part of our own experience. The difficulty arises when we try to understand how in the last analysis people look upon life and death. And at this point it seems precarious, if not impossible to call on common understanding and experience.

There are three issues here:
1. the 'consolation of the Church' certainly does not imply telling the patient how he or she ought to feel;
2. the 'consolation of the Church' consists in the communion that develops when we tell each other how we really feel;
3. this communion can be celebrated and stimulated through the rites of the sacraments.

In connection with this we shall have to discuss—and this is most important—whether and how this communion can give consolation to those who do not feel themselves linked to the Church through faith.

First let us look at what certainly does *not* constitute the
'consolation of the Church'. In the previous chapter I said
that pastoral care for the dying is only secondarily a
task for professionals and is primarily a task for lay people.
Is this conviction idealistic or theoretical? To my mind it is
eminently practical. It is certainly true that many sick and
dying people fail to get what they need, but this is an unhealthy and unsatisfactory situation. We have learned to
resign ourselves to the fact that in our mutual relationships
we keep silent, we lie and let each other down, helplessly and
with a bad conscience. We have got used to the fact that 'of
course we can't speak about our faith and our deepest
experiences.' When we do talk about our faith then all too
often it becomes more like a controversial exchange than
anything else, and we have had more than enough of this.
We do not manage to present our faith and our confidence—
so far as they exist—in a refreshing, liberating way. All this
is certainly an unhealthy taste of affairs. And we cannot
solve these problems just by calling in the professionals.
Commonsense is not the prerogative of psychologists, a
healthy faith is not the privilege of the theologian. On the
contrary, the establishment of normal human relationships
is a task for every one of us and a sound community of faith
can only be created by 'lay people' who are able to communicate with one another about their faith. No community
of faith is going to be created if professionals keep nagging
about religious convictions which remain alien to their
deepest experiences. A deep misgiving exists among us that
in talking together we will each force our own religious
beliefs and experiences upon the other. Thus a doctor once
told me frankly that he kept priests and ministers away from
dying Christian patients for as long as he possibly could.
'These priests,' he said, 'will talk a young man into resig-
nation while he is full of protest and revolt at his situation.
Let him revolt. For God's sake, let him revolt.' The doctor
is right. Freud, Klein and Lindemann have all spoken about
the anger felt by a man faced with death and the tremendous

effort it takes the patient to work through these profound emotions.[2] The doctor is right. For God's sake, let the sick man give vent to his feelings of anger and revolt. And yet the doctor is not absolutely right.

The 'consolation of the Church' means going to that young patient and letting him hear that you understand how he feels, how he wants to say to God, 'My God, my God, you have let me down, damn it!' This is not very different from Christ's words on the cross, when he began to say Psalm 22. Thus you don't benumb the feelings of this young man, you give him the chance to share his feelings and memories, his doubts and hopes, his fears and his joys, not with uninvolved professionals but with people who love him so much that his feelings reverberate in the depth and richness of their own.

But is it possible for laymen to do this, or am I presupposing a language which only ministers have at their disposal? I think that in this matter we ought to make demands upon each other, layman and priest alike. Paul Pruyser[3] points out how we fail to make use of our own heritage and he supports the growing protest against the shallow, superficial language which is used by Christians, not excluding priests, in their contacts with the sick. Perhaps by now we have got out of the habit of imposing our own feelings on each other. At least we have grown careful in this respect, which is good. But at the same time we have made the contacts between us so much more impoverished and shallow. We should stop neglecting the means by which our feelings can be expressed and shared: praying, reading aloud, laying on of hands, blessing and anointing, feeding each other with the sacrament of the Eucharist. If we do these things, we are offering our dying friends something more than ourselves and our poor limited feelings: we are bringing them in contact with the age-long life of the Church, in all its richness.

Can lay people do this? I believe that if need be, they can learn how. Here are two instances of lay people who were able to bring 'the consolation of the Church' to someone else. A friend of mine went to see an acquaintance of his who was close to death. As the man was alternately semi-conscious and unconscious it was hard to make any contact with him.Then my friend hit on the idea of bringing a tape recorder with him. He sat for hours beside the patient, and at intervals he played Gregorian music because he knew how dear it had always been to his dying friend. Before long it became clear from the expression on his face and his general attitude that the sick man found both relief and comfort in the familiar chant. Quite different is the example of a Protestant doctor who used to visit his Catholic friend in hospital. He never took leave of his friend without laying hands on him. The sick man himself told me how much benefit this gesture brought him.

The mediation of a priest or minister is professional. He can only do this noble task if he is willing to go on learning. I think that the first task of a priest is to learn the art of understanding and translating the sick man's feelings and also of translating them into religious language, if this is to the benefit of the patient.

Kastenbaum[4] sketches two types of clergymen who will never learn to do this. The first one 'entered the sick room of a woman while she was recovering from major surgery. He smilingly asked her how she was feeling. Before she could begin to reply, he was commenting on the weather. He announced that he was compiling a list of people who wanted to receive Holy Communion the following morning. As she began to form the reply on her dry lips, he had already commented on the flowers at the foot of the bed and disappeared through the door in order to inflict himself upon as many other sufferers as possible.' The other extreme, according to Kastenbaum, is represented by the minister who walks into the sick room with a prayer book or Bible clenched tightly in his hand. He has already decided what he will read, what prayers he will say, what questions he will ask and what topics he will avoid. This minister has taken pains to prepare himself for the visit. Nothing will find him at a loss, nothing take him by surprise, disturb him or take him out of his depth. This minister came just to do a job. But that is not pastoral work. Pastoral care always means entering into the feelings of the other so that we do not 'cover up' but lay open. Even more, it means listening to and looking at what is being revealed.

I once heard something very impressive when I visited a patient in a clinic where I had formerly worked. This man, who was in a general ward in the University Hospital in Utrecht, told me how much he envied the other patients who were Protestants. He himself used to be visited by the Catholic priest who, one could say, merely dropped in now and then for a chat. But his Protestant friends were visited by a minister who not only talked with them but who ended with prayer. And there he lay, some distance away, listening enviously to this prayer which accurately expressed the deep feelings of his companions.

We hope that the days are over when the Catholic priest simply dropped in for a chat, offered some slight distraction, and finally gave a blessing and left. We are gradually learning, priest and patient, to pray together; and we are also beginning to realise that prayer is quite beside the mark unless it expresses what has just been talked about. I remember a sick man who was in an angry, complaining mood when I went to see him. His miseries poured out—he kept telling me how desperate he felt, how he was deserted by everybody, how he didn't want to die, how horrible it was to die young. Then he said roughly 'Go on, what are you waiting for? Go ahead, and say a prayer.' It seemed to me that I ought to start with 'My God, my God, why have you forsaken me?' Then he interrupted me scornfully. 'No!' he said, 'it's not as bad as *that*!' So then we said Psalm 91 together: 'He who dwells in the shelter of the Most High says to the Lord, my refuge, my stronghold, my God in whom I trust.'

While we were finding this prayer we discovered between

us that all his anger and complaining had really to be interpreted as a plea for security, a plea to trust and to be trusted.
In other words, our praying together not only strengthened
the relationship that had grown up between us and raised it
to God but at the same time our search for contact and
communication was tested, purified and celebrated.

It is only in the sacraments that this celebration reaches
its fullness. But before discussing this we have to answer the
question: 'What do we do with our faith when confronted
with death?'

3

What do we do with our faith when confronted with death?

DURING the German occupation of Holland a group of prominent theologians, Catholic and Protestant, produced a book called *What do they Believe?*[1] It indicated the interest of each group in the other's faith and it considered such questions as: Are our ways of believing different? How do we resemble each other? How do we differ? Both groups were curious as to what divided them, particularly with regard to the content of faith. The content of faith remains important of course, but it is typical that today our interests have moved into a rather different field. We also want answers to questions like these: 'What are we doing with this faith of ours? What do we want to achieve with it? What do we expect from it?' These are certainly pastoral questions. St James has already pointed to them in his epistle: 'You believe that God is one; you do well. Even the demons believe and shudder.'[2]

One would like to know therefore how priests throughout the centuries have dealt with the question 'What are we doing with our faith?' when they were in contact with the dying. Van Laarhoven and Zandbelt have pointed out with astonishment that writings on the history of the Church have absolutely nothing to offer on this subject.[3] We know that priests went out to administer the last sacraments, that they tried to prepare the sick to receive the sacraments fittingly, with feelings of contrition, humility, confidence and gratitude. But it is a fact that only in recent times has 'the personal religious attitude of the person receiving the sacrament become much more central.'[4] This shift in theological interest is clearly related to the whole change in our interest in one another as human persons. This change, this anthropocentric shift[5] is expressed in and also stimulated by all the various forms of welfare and social

15

services. The question 'What do people do with their faith
when confronted with death?' has been raised most forcibly
by those who offer psychotherapeutic help to the dying. In
Holland A. van Dantzig has written about the psychology
of the fear of death[6] and he has built up considerable
experience through helping people in the grip of this mortal
fear. He believes that their fear of death is a fear of living.
They have not learned during their lifetime how to cope
with loneliness, how to accept failure. They feel that important elements in their lives have never come to fulfilment.
This loneliness torments them, this feeling of dependence
makes them fearful of death. It is only possible for me to
accept my death if I can accept my life as it has actually been.
I may have made others unhappy, I may have failed to
grasp important opportunities, now I long for somebody to
hold my hand, and there is nobody. I can only die at peace
when I have faced up to this, when I have accepted the actual
course of my life. In van Dantzig's opinion this acceptance of
self becomes increasingly difficult, impossible almost,
precisely because people do have faith. For after all, he says,
how does a believer look at death, what does he believe?
Isn't it something like this?

1. 'I needn't be afraid of unfulfilment. Life isn't taken
   away, it's only changed.[7] Life isn't finished yet; a further
   purification, purgatory, will follow.' But meanwhile we
   are so complicated that we go on fearing death.

2. 'I needn't fear loneliness. After all 'the Lord is my
   shepherd, there is nothing I shall want'.[8] And 'into your
   hands I commend my spirit'.[9] But despite this faith or
   just because of it some dying people remain full of fear.
   For at the same time they are also thinking about the
   terrifying judgement that is coming when their every
   action will be disclosed. For we have certainly been
   conditioned to imagine ourselves quailing before the
   judge who will open the book,—

'Lo, the book exactly worded
Wherein all has been recorded
Thence shall judgment be awarded.'[10]

Here I am filling out the sober words of the psychotherapist with the imagery handed down to the faithful through
preaching, liturgy and catechesis. Of course more than this
has been handed down—confidence, joy and the radiant
face of Jesus. Still it is certain that as Christians we don't
realise how our faith conditions us; we are not good at
observing ourselves and realising how we are affected by its
religious imagery and language. The psychotherapist has
good reason to believe that many dying people fail to overcome their fear and cover it up with vague beliefs, with what
looks rather like a common delusion. To be more precise—
we are afraid of death, we don't want to die. So we invent
one world after this one in which all our fears find place,
the world of hell; and we invent a better world after this one,
the world of heaven, where all our wishes find fulfilment.
As long as we do this we have not started on the difficult
exploration of our innermost self and we do not resolve our
fears. And this is a pity because it would seem that a dying
man who can, even at the very end, look closely at himself
and accept himself is able to die in peace, in surrender.
'Reality, once it has been faced, seems bearable, even
desirable.'[11]

Lastly there is the danger that whoever tries to help the
dying patient may find his own faith a handicap which
prevents him from being really interested in the patient; or
at least his faith may give him an excuse for his lack of
contact. I have not often observed this in those who counsel
the dying, but I have seen it only too often in those who try
to comfort the bereaved. They make facile references to the
happiness of the dead man now that he is with God. This
gives them an excuse to be less involved in the grief of the
relatives, in whose presence they feel at a loss or for whom
they have no time to spare.

Summing up, Van Dantzig remarks that faith offered no

solution, either individual or collective, to the patients he
was in touch with because:

—it is an impersonal solution;
—it habitually presents God as someone who counts my
'sins' and demands retribution;
—it glosses over death;
—it provides an excuse for defective relationships;
—but above all, it fosters a childish self-centredness.
Believers of this kind still see themselves as the centre
of the universe, with sun, moon and stars bowing down
to them.[12] They cannot imagine the world going on
without them.

Here we touch upon the way in which humanists try to
assist the dying. It has been formulated, among others by
Lips.[13] Humanist counsellors realise that they must help
people to accept their own finiteness, to be open to whatever
is going to happen, to take responsibility for their own
decisions about their lives, in short to overcome their fear
through responsibility and humanity. These observations
are of great importance in counselling the dying. They help
to elucidate the question: 'What are we doing with our
faith?' They shed light therefore on the objectives of
counselling the dying; they also have something important
to offer towards the discussion of how and whether there
could and should be co-operation between Christian ministers and humanist counsellors.

The faithful have not been unaffected by the increased
knowledge derived from pastoral care for the dying and by
humanist observations on it. The number of these who
believe in the hereafter is decreasing; believers find their
faith challenged far more than it used to be. Moreover
theologians are being urged for the good of everyone to
offer adequate formulas for belief in resurrection and—
which is not the same thing—to justify it.[14] The language of
the liturgy and the way it is carried out have been revised.
The themes of light and peace have been retained, belief in
Christ's resurrection had been afforded the fullest attention,

while judgment and its grim medieval interpretation in the
Dies Irae, have been pushed into the background.[15] Now
the emphasis is placed on liberation from sin.[16] It is precisely the problem of death which has made so many people
lose their faith or declare its invalidity or try to formulate it
more clearly. All this still only gives a partial answer to the
question: 'What do people do with their faith when confronted with death?' A more precise answer might be
something like this: in meeting with death our faith can
indeed be abused and made to protect our egocentricity or
anxiety. Nevertheless it is also true that impending death
brings about a crisis in which ultimately it becomes possible
for us to give up our self-defences and learn to make a final
genuine surrender, If we can do this then our faith will
finally and definitely acquire the theological and psychological character of authentic religious faith. Miskotte[17]
puts it like this: 'Our faith, as faith, is taken away from us.
We can no longer justify our believing; we have no basis left.
This is the secret which both devastates and saves us.'
Erikson[18] uses more down to earth language to describe
this process and says that the first step towards a more
authentic faith consists in becoming convinced that one is
not God. The process of dying is a purification of our faith.
We make the final discovery that, after all, things will go
on in the world without us. At long last one gets the chance
to surrender oneself to a mystery for which this self 'has
neither power nor words, unless the mysterious words of
faith.' The believer enters death as he enters a dark night, to
use the imagery of St John of the Cross. In a similar way
H. Berkof[19] describes the Christian state of mind as a more
or less ambivalent mixture of fear and expectation: 'I have
the impression that expectation gets the better of fear as
expectation flowers into unconditional surrender.'

It is a well-known fact that when people bear witness to
their faith they generally do so with a mixture of confidence
and anxious defensiveness, whether of themselves or of the
Church. In the light of this, any unequivocal pronouncement

concerning faith makes less impression on us. But it is moving to find a tangled mixture of these characteristics in the testimony of a woman who had heard from the surgeon that she had only a few more weeks to live. She said: 'What is so strange is that from that very moment I began to get much calmer. I knew then what I'd got to start thinking about, what feelings I'd got to cope with. And it was only then, I'd say, only then, that I really felt the fullness, the richness of faith. It may sound odd perhaps but since then we haven't had a single moment of gloom. We've enjoyed ourselves just as we always have done. I'm only forty-three so I'd expected a lot more from life. I've enjoyed life and I've lived a full life. I've loved all the everyday contacts with people too. . . . If I didn't have faith as strong as a rock I'm certain I wouldn't accept it. I'd kick against the situation. I'd want to hang on to life. But now I can offer my life back to God, as it were, and get something far more beautiful in return.'[20] This woman tells what she experiences in this last phase of her life: a joy at feeling herself to be a significant part of the universe,[21] a feeling of security too deep to describe, a new meaning in all her ordinary day to day relationships. And yet alongside this she feels a sort of rebellion which must be overpowered by a faith 'firm as a rock.' Peter Hofstede was deeply impressed by this brave woman, as were all those around her. Nevertheless she might have become more mature and the message she wanted to convey might have carried even more conviction if her feelings of revolt had been openly expressed and resolved. Had this taken place she would not have made the mistake of saying that people without faith always want to cling to life.

Pastoral care for the dying means helping us to use our faith, no longer to protect ourselves, but really to surrender. In the case of this woman, it means that someone should have helped her to express all the feelings of revolt she was warding off. Someone should have given her the security of knowing that it wasn't her faith that was firm as a rock; that it is the Lord who is the rock and our refuge. Probably she would have discovered that this, in the last analysis, was what she had meant to say. She would have come into closer contact with her deepest experiences and longings; she would have been less hampered by what still remained of anxiety and fear.

4

The people around the dying patient

PETER HOFSTEDE[1] quotes part of a letter from a boy of seventeen who knows that he will die before long. 'You should just look at the faces of people who haven't seen you for some time: they've made their minds up in advance to be jolly and hearty and cheer you up. They bring you flowers and fruit—peaches for instance, which I can't stand! Then all of a sudden they see you. Their artificial smile freezes into a sort of stony grin; there's a flash of panic and disgust and fear in their eyes. They'd much rather run away once they've dropped the fruit and flowers on your bed because they find you repulsive. They hardly dare to look at you. It's only the very strong ones who can stand it, just to stay sitting with you.'

Harrie Nouwen[2] has described a similar situation, involving a young soldier who had been badly wounded. When he spoke of the priests who visited him in the military hospital, he saw how ill at ease and uncertain they were, and how they tried to hide this by forced joviality and superficial chat.

It is useful to learn what impression we make on people who are bedridden or dying. In an ingenious way Le Shan[3] has confronted nurses with the unconscious delays they make on their way to the dying person's bed. Kastenbaum and Aisenberg[4] write about a psychiatrist, a physician, a clergyman and a social psychologist, each of whom commented independently on a report on counselling the dying. They were unanimous on the following points:

1. we tend to put the dying person in emotional isolation;
2. we tend to treat him in a routine way;
3. we tend to treat him as though he were a child, unable to take any responsibility or to cope with his situation on an adult level;

22

4. those who are intimately involved with him do not communicate adequately;
5. they also fail to recognise and fulfil their share of the total responsibility.

So we make organisational mistakes, but these are the consequences of the emotional problems we have about people who are dying. Because of this a great dividing wall exists between the healthy and the dying, and it is the healthy who build this wall and keep it in existence; the sick do not belong any more.

According to the four experts mentioned above we act in this way because we believe that dying people are inferior to ourselves, inferior that is, simply because they are dying. A dying man is someone in process of becoming a failure.[5] We also keep up the wall between us because we have never learned how to deal with the dying and it is most unpleasant to find ourselves in a situation we cannot cope with. But above all, it is our own insecurity and fear that are brought to the surface and fill us with apprehension. Leonard Pearson[6] tells a significant story in this connection. He was conducting group therapy in a home for old people and one day a member of the group failed to appear. He asked the reason why. His assistant, embarrassed, said that he would tell him about it later! But another member of the group said calmly, 'He died last night.' This incident led to a useful exchange of feelings about death. But at a subsequent meeting of the staff there was considerable reluctance to discuss the subject. Before long Pearson felt himself becoming isolated among the staff, the object of curious interest. People came to look on him as an expert in death and dying and they kept well away from him.

Pastoral care for the dying must therefore bring some healing element into our mutual deception, under-valuation, isolation and routine, stereotyped behaviour. One important remedy could lie in the recognition and discussion of such behaviour. If we do act towards the dying in the way described above then it is a real service when someone helps us to see our clumsiness and to accept it. This does not mean that we have already learned to act in a better way but we have at least been made aware of our ignorance and our desire to learn has been awakened.

One important element in the contacts between healthy and dying people is the powerlessness which seizes them both when they want to express their love and care for each other, and their grief at the impending separation. Here is one account of such a situation.[7]

Mr E. was in the final stage of cancer. He was alone in a hospital room where practically no one visited him except his wife. He was ignorant of the gravity of his illness but he felt desperately ill. He was a Catholic and had already talked once or twice with the priest. The latter chanced to visit him one day when his wife was present. They had not met before so they shook hands and the wife told the priest how much she had already heard about him. The sick man told them that he felt frightful, that he could hardly speak, could barely breathe. Then his wife began to pour out her heart. 'How terrible it is! He wants to gets better so much, just look how ill he is. He's only sixty-nine, he was just going to retire and then his whole life would have been easier. Now he can't breathe and they can't do anything about it. We've always got on well together, we've loved each other so much. In God's name why does this have to happen to us?' The priest began to reply when suddenly the sick man interrupted him: 'Father,' he said, 'am I going to die?' At this the wife fled from the room. The priest asked: 'Would it upset you very much if you were?' The man said, 'Well, I think it would be terrible for my wife. Sometimes I feel like kicking against it all. I'd like you to pray a bit. It's difficult for me to pray properly.'

At this point the priest suggested that they should pray together, all three of them. The wife stood outside in the corridor weeping, saying that she didn't know what to do next. Together she and the priest returned. Stricken with grief, the husband and wife looked at one another, and took each other by the hand. 'If only I could do something for you,' said the wife. Then the priest prayed: 'God our Father,' he said, 'here we are in your presence and there is nothing we can do. We can only come to you with our sorrow. . . . Be close to us, God, especially in these difficult moments.' The priest promised to return soon and he was back within a week. The nurses then told him that the patient still had no idea that he was close to death and they lacked the courage to tell him. This time the patient was in a worse state than ever. 'You are suffering a lot aren't you?' The man nodded his head and asked: 'Am I going to die, Father?' 'You realise, don't you, that you are very ill indeed?' Again he nodded. 'So there is a very real possibility that you may die.' The sick man stared fixedly at the priest. 'Does this make you feel very sad now?' The man shook his head in emphatic denial, and said: 'I believe that everything will work out for the best.' He clasped his hands together and the priest said a short prayer with him. A few days later the priest went to the hospital again. Meanwhile the doctor had told the wife that her husband's death was imminent and husband and wife had talked about it together. The priest said: 'You are in great pain aren't you, but I believe that you are much calmer than you were.' 'Yes, so much has happened,' the sick man replied, 'my wife and I both know now that I'm going to die soon. It's strange but everything is different now.' 'You are more relaxed, in spite of your breathlessness and pain.' The man nodded. Then he told the priest how he had rebelled against his situation, still the priest shouldn't blame him for that, he said. But now he was much more at peace. Then the priest continued: 'Because you've talked with your wife, because you know this pain is going to end, that everything will work out for the best.' 'I'd looked forward to retiring,' said the sick man, 'well, I'm going to start my retirement now. In my better moments the only thing I ask for is to see God soon. How lonely people must be who don't do anything about their faith. . . . '

This summary account of the meetings is interesting for several reasons. The patient himself asked if he was going to die. In spite of this he only 'really knew' this after his talk with his wife. Before that he hovered between hope and fear, between wanting to know and denying, in the state which Hacker and Weismann call 'middle knowledge'.[8] 'Only in the security of his relationship with his wife was the patient given the opportunity really to take in this information and assimilate it.'[9] And in order to be able to assimilate this knowledge about death the dying man had to share it with his wife. The priest therefore, acted as intermediary between husband and wife. They had been married 'for better, for worse' and therefore they had to accept that when one suffers, the other suffers. The husband had not accepted his feelings of revolt against his situation. When the priest tried to help him to express this rebellion in his prayer he invited husband and wife to pray together. They took each other by the hand. When I read the report I was struck by this gesture. People remember the day of their wedding when they took each other's hand in a solemn gesture. Here the gesture was repeated. 'What therefore God has joined together, let no man put asunder'[10] not by one single sorrow, still less by helplessness. Imminent death threatened to separate them; but now that they could talk about it and could exchange their feelings of revolt and distress, now they became willing to say goodbye. At the same time it is clear that faith does not cover up anything; the experience of faith is an element in the re-establishing of contact and only then does it become an element of a hope which reaches beyond death. 'I . . . believe that everything will work out for the best. I'm going to start my retirement now.' And on the basis of this restored fundamental confidence he felt compassion for those 'who have no hope.'[11]

In cases where dying is protracted it may happen that these restored and deepened relationships can be experienced in a more relaxed way. I myself have sat beside a dying woman with her husband and children while we ate cakes as a birthday celebration. Nothing was covered up on that occasion. The atmosphere was one of affection, jokes and good natured teasing. I have also heard a woman discuss with her sick husband all the details of his funeral, the colour of the flowers, the clothes she would wear, while he joked with her, saying that he only regretted that he wouldn't be able to admire her on the day.

It is clear that the better communication is restored and deepened the better the sacraments can be celebrated: the last anointing and the Eucharist. Here a human encounter is given a spiritual depth. 'Where two or three are gathered together in my name, there am I in the midst of them.'[12] Still, I cannot finish this chapter on the contacts between the dying person and those around him without the following pastoral remarks.

In spite of all that has been said above we should not forget that it is up to the patient to decide how much he wants to share and with whom.

There are people who want to receive the last sacraments with nobody present except the priest. A patient who asked me to give him the sacrament on the following day refused most explicitly to have anyone else present: 'I'm going to tell everyone that this isn't a show for the public.' Another man wanted only his wife and no other member of his family. Others again specify exactly who they want to invite, though most patients leave it to circumstances to decide. The point is that there should be an atmosphere in which all who are present, and in particular the sick man himself, can express their deepest emotions. The sacrament is curative, at least in the sense that it helps to purify our feelings, to achieve what in psychotherapy is called catharsis. I once found a most moving instance of this[13] when the sacrament was given to a priest suffering from complete loss of speech, *motor aphasia*, caused by dissemination of a lung tumour into the brain. The situation was truly pitiful because the patient could barely express his feelings, literally he couldn't find words. He had been a strong man of vehement feelings, a good preacher and spiritual guide, a man who had never been afraid of speaking his mind to his parishioners. He had been anointed, he had listened to the prayers and he was about to receive communion. We prayed (in Latin as we still did at that time), 'Lord I am not worthy: Domine non sum dignus.' And then all of a sudden after weeks of silence he spoke again, 'Non sum dignus.'

It is a well known fact that people suffering from motor aphasia can sometimes suddenly find words to express their feelings. Here we heard the words with which this man expressed his relationship with God, words full of self knowledge and self surrender.

For patients who are seriously ill or dying the sacraments can be the crown set on their deepest feelings of belonging— and these can also restore these feelings. But then the celebration of the sacraments really has to be based on something shared, upon a relationship between the patient and the community of which the priest is the representative.[14] This does not happen if a patient discovers that he has already been given the sacrament before he had the chance of saying 'Yes' or 'No'. It may well be that patients who say that this is what happened to them tell exaggerated stories. All the same it proves that in every case they were so uninvolved in the preparations that no genuine celebration took place, still less any encouragement to their personal development.

5

The things that are discussed

WHAT do they talk about, the dying person and the one who gives him pastoral help? Going through my notes I can answer in one word: 'Everything'. In this chapter I shall try to put this 'everything' into some sort of order.

People talk about their life history, the problems they have never managed to solve, how they feel about their physical decline, and about parting. They express gratitude for life, and astonishment that there is still so much left to experience, they talk about faith and doubt and how these fluctuate when you come face to face with death. Thus they talk about their past, their present, their future. Sometimes these subjects are broached in connection with their struggle to accept impending death and they illustrate the successive and alternating stages in a patient's adaptation. Kübler-Ross[1] has described this for America and J. Michels[2] for the Netherlands. This chapter therefore is not intended to make any corrective on the information they give us. Rather it is meant to draw the reader's attention to the unexpected richness inherent in the contacts with someone who is dying.

1 The personal life history
It seems that on his own level, every dying person wants to construct his 'self-portrait' in the form of a jigsaw puzzle.[3] Dying people feel the need to retell large parts of their life history, what their parents were like, the sort of education they had, how they got married, the important decisions they made and sometimes went back on. They speak about their work, their children, their colleagues and the people they have looked after. And almost all of them also talk about their religious life, the vicissitudes of their faith, the history of their religious feelings, and the influence of

husband or wife on these feelings. The development of their illness is also discussed and how they experienced its first symptoms. A woman patient told me what an important role her husband had played in helping her to overcome her fear and keep her self-confidence and how this had resulted in bettering her relations with her children. When one of her breasts had to be removed she had been afraid that her husband would find her less attractive and would love her less. But he had given her every opportunity to talk about her fear and so the threat to her self-confidence had been warded off. He had neither dismissed her fear nor minimised it but had helped her to look at it and overcome it. The self-portrait is like a jigsaw puzzle. Whether the pieces are put together rapidly or slowly will obviously depend on the time and energy that remain. Sometimes a patient needs only a few sentences to sketch himself and his life. Sometimes these lines are so characteristic of the man that they can be used as a basis for talks with the bereaved family.

This pre-occupation with the self-portrait can best be described as a search for a certain harmony and wholeness—the jigsaw puzzle, 'this is what I am like now'. This final self-exploration is the last and decisive phase in personal development. It is concerned with making a cohesive wholeness of life. It is also decisive for overcoming the fear of death. 'This fear of death testifies that the person concerned has not accepted the individual and unique course of his life as the best thing that life could offer.'[4] Such an achievement is only possible when the patient has learnt how to deal with his failures, his guilt and his unresolved problems.

2 The unresolved problems

Practically every patient also tells about conflicts that were never solved, fears which have never been completely overcome, sexual problems that were only partly resolved. People speak about the things they would still have liked to do, countries they would have liked to visit or go back to.

Finding it hard to accept death means finding it hard to accept the unfinished: 'If only I could have written this or that; if only I could have gone on that journey, if I could only see the spring next year! I wish I could have been better to my wife, my husband. I wish I could have been more tolerant. But some things just didn't work out.' These are subjects for 'confession', they are also subjects to which feelings of guilt can cling. Van der Klei points out that it is bad pastoral practice to minimise such feelings. This holds good for any feelings but particularly for feelings of guilt. Because what it really amounts to is a refusal to make contact since my 'pastoral reassurance' leaves the sick man alone with his guilt feelings, which anyway I have probably covered up. Yet is it not a pastoral ministry to proclaim God's forgiveness and to be a channel of it? I think that the actual pastoral task consists in helping each other to accept God's forgiveness. This means aiding each other to work through feelings of guilt instead of saying that there is no reason to feel them. To listen with acceptance, and without prejudice or judgement to the 'confession' of guilt feelings is to express our Christian confidence that the 'truly necessary sin of Adam' has been blotted out by Christ's death. These words of the Easter hymn 'the truly necessary sin of Adam'[6] may seem shocking but they reveal to us that we shall never find out what we really are if we are not prepared to say that this crime, this murder, this adultery, this dishonesty, was necessary for me in order to find out what sort of person I was and what my personal way of conversion and change must be. It is the authentic practical way in which I find out, not what sort of general sinner I was, but what sort of redeemable person I am. And when we make this discovery we can realise the meaning of the words ' "into your hands I commend my spirit", my self!'

Such a 'confession' may conclude in a variety of ways—in praying together, in looking at a crucifix, in pronouncing and listening to the words of absolution. But equally it may end with the sick man saying something like 'I'm glad to get this off my chest. It's made me feel much better. Now I think I can put up with getting weaker.'

3 The experience of physical decline

In talking about increasing bodily weakness two themes are paramount. First: 'How I hate the thought of turning into a corpse'; second 'It's so hard to accept that I'm becoming more and more of a burden to everyone. For me the big question is how I'm going to die with any dignity when every day I lose more dignity.'

In the image we have of ourselves the body plays an important part. It is through our body that we appear to others and to ourselves: in our body that we notice what we can or cannot still do. The dying man is likely to find his body steadily becoming less and less of an instrument and more and more of a wreck, a prison which renders him helpless and puts him into the hands of others, no longer beautiful or a thing to be proud of, a burden, something no longer lovable. As the body fails, it threatens to break the existing relationships of love and friendship. Here too it is inadvisable to minimise these complaints. The sick man has to learn to accept that he is a burden and that we have to bear this burden together. It is in this context that the question of euthanasia may arise. If it has been raised by the patient then it must also be considered in what we call the 'pastoral encounter'. Now I agree with Sporken[7] that the question of euthanasia is not raised as frequently as the mass media would have us believe. The public discussion about it is more like an exercise in thinking without prejudice. And I also agree that to discuss euthanasia is by no means always the same thing as to ask for it. Rather it is a cry for help, a plea for *faithfulness* in the pastoral relationship. 'Now that you have talked to me about my death you mustn't leave me in the lurch. If you have to go away I want to know when you'll come back again.' I think that in certain circumstances this may even imply that the pastor must postpone, even indefinitely, any holiday or absence no matter how much he may feel the need to relax and rest. We ought to be suspicious if the question of euthanasia is never raised in a pastoral encounter; or to put it more exactly, if a minister were to say that such topics are never mentioned when he visits the sick. For it could give reason for supposing that certain topics just can't be discussed with this particular cleric. Pastoral help doesn't consist in reiterating the commandments but guiding people towards the freedom of their own choices. This means thinking with them, feeling with them, helping them to overcome their fear. It also means recognising that given present day medical resources the question may really arise as to whether the process of dying, if it is very much protracted, may in fact be detrimental to dying with human dignity. This can become a serious question; it is one of the new decisions which people are probably going to have to face. Priests then ought not to leave their patients in the lurch because 'all who labour and are heavily burdened should be able to come to Him.'[8] They should help their patients to make their decision with as much trust, lucidity of mind and surrender to God as possible. It is not certain that God will invariably tell a person that he must choose duration rather than human dignity. Sometimes I could wish that the public statements of church leaders on this subject could be less general and abstract, less defensive, and could offer more practical help. This would, I believe, be for the real good of many.

4 Parting

It is difficult to feel and to describe with any accuracy what dying people experience when they have to part from those they love. Their feelings undergo change during the various stages in the process of dying. It is my opinion however that even those who have accepted death still suffer deep sorrow at the separation. 'It's not dying that's so awful, what I can't bear is the parting.' All sorts of feelings come into play here —the pain of having to let go, anxiety about the loved ones, worry about what the sick man himself can do to comfort those who will be left behind. But we should make a distinction between the experience of people who are saying goodbye and what pastoral help implies here. In the first place a very sick man will find it easier to take leave of his relatives if he can give expression to the pain and sorrow of it to whoever is giving him pastoral help. Besides it is a great support if he can feel that the one caring for him will also, if need be, care for those he has to part from. Whether such confidence can really develop will depend on the depth of the relationship that has grown up between patient and pastor. But it will also depend on the extent of the priest's general experience in pastoral counselling. The dying know too that the 'consolation of the Church' extended to their relatives ceases all to often at their funeral. Perhaps we need to learn anew how to help the bereaved; so making it easier for the dying man to say goodbye to this life with greater confidence.

Is the distress that surrounds this parting alleviated by the hope of meeting again in the hereafter? The Christian's goodbye should be 'a valediction forbidding mourning' (John Donne); because they can make their own the words of the old revivalist hymn:

> 'Yes we'll gather at the river,
>   the beautiful, the beautiful river;
>   gather with the saints at the river
>   that flows by the throne of God.'

But those who are left behind have still to learn a lesson. They have to learn to let go: 'they shouldn't envy their son heaven' as it is put in a 17th century Dutch poem. They must believe and hope, recognising with Guiderius in Cymbeline that

> 'thou thy worldly task hast done,
>   home art gone and ta'en thy wages.'

This letting go, this liberation of self, this leave taking is one thing for the grieving family, another for the man or woman who is dying. Seriously ill people certainly feel deep sorrow but also the relief of letting go.

A young woman suffering from a serious internal disease had been told by her doctor that it was incurable. Everything was done to keep her out of hospital and on her own feet as long as possible. When I talked with her for the first time she was clearly aware of her condition but she was worried about her children. She found it hard that before long she would have to leave them to the sole care of her husband. Six months later she still had the same worry but by now she had accepted the situation. 'I must', she said realistically, 'I have to resign myself to the fact that I just can't do it any more.'

And about meeting again in the hereafter? I have the impression that this is a consolation for the living. The dying have to pass through the dark tunnel of death alone, having said goodbye. I believe that they can achieve this more easily if their gratitude for life is able to blossom into hope and confidence.

5 Gratitude and hope

Many people die whose lives up till then seem to provide little reason for gratitude. Examples are not hard to find. Here is one.[9] Mr L was a man of about forty, who had spent more than six months in hospital. As a result of trachectomy, a necessary operation on his windpipe, he could not speak. He communicated by writing with a pen on a writing pad. During these six months the priest visited him three times. Between the first and second visits several months elapsed, between the second and third only a few weeks. During the first visit the man wrote with heavy underlining that the whole place was a mess, the hospital authorities were a worse mess and the clergy of course couldn't even see this. The priest suggested that the man should write what he considered the worst aspect of all this. 'They don't do anything for me' the man wrote. 'Here I am thirty-four weeks in hospital. No one helps me and I can't do anything.' The priest tried to get him to reflect. 'I suppose this must be very difficult for you, I'm trying to think with you, to feel how you feel. I'm sure you do need help—but where's it got to come from?' At this the sick man wrote, 'Are you saying I've got to help myself?' Whilst the priest was taking the greatest care in agreeing with this the sick man flew into a fury, indicated that the priest had better clear out, and flung the pen from the bed. At the second visit the patient seemed to be struggling to accept his own helplessness, and at the end of the conversation he expressly thanked the priest. At the third visit he seemed at peace. 'Had a lot to learn,' he wrote. 'See life differently now. Business affairs settled, wife taken care of. Some things still to be arranged but I'm satisfied now.' The priest agreed and the man wrote on: 'Grateful to you, I haven't prayed for years. Can't do it now either. You do it for me. Don't think it means nothing to me. I want to land up in the right place.'

The man himself and those around him have both contributed to this change from rebelling to gratitude. Those around him have seen to it that his worries as husband and father have been alleviated. He himself has struggled to learn to live with his helplessness and his terrible handicap and he is explicitly grateful to the priest because the latter started him off on this process of working through his problem. There is little to be thankful for, only the encouragement 'to take up your cross and carry it'. All the same the man is grateful and now he would like the relationship between him and the priest to be developed into a sort of vicarious praying because he 'wants to land up in the right place'. Dying people it seems can become grateful for their damaged lives and this gratitude turns into a sense of belonging, a feeling seen and described by Rümke[10] that 'one is significantly linked with the universe.' Mr L had not yet reached that stage. He had undergone a change which could be described quite simply, quite ordinarily, as resigning himself to the inevitable. But there was more to it than that. He had learned this by resorting to his own possibilities. He had recovered the courage to look at himself again. And he was grateful for it. In this mood of introspection and gratitude he wanted 'to land in the right place', to be reunited with God who was once more going to be his hope and his future. For God does not simply reconcile, he also becomes everything and is in everything, even for Mr L.

6 So much still remains

In describing dying people am I raising them to such a high level of experience that we ordinary people can never hope to reach it? I can well understand the suspicion that to describe the process of dying from a pastoral angle tends to surround the patients with the 'fragrance of holiness' and can make them seem like saints. What shall I say to this? I genuinely believe that in the process of dying a man is given the opportunity to achieve a level of maturity that was impossible in the past either because the opportunities were lacking or because he failed to make use of them. In this context I too have witnessed deaths which were talked about long afterwards. I think that this is what was called in earlier days 'a happy death'. Such a death was something to long for. In the litany of the saints, that great prayer of intercession, one prayed 'from sudden and unprovided death, deliver us Lord.' Such a 'happy death' has been described by Van Es when he was asked how he would wish to die: fully conscious, he said, in the midst of his loved ones, well prepared, all the important things having been said beforehand.[11] All the same a 'happy death' is still a natural human death. This is indicated by the very natural experiences and events which still occur. Van der Meer[12] makes a plea that we should not draw the curtains in the sick room; it must always be possible to look out at the world. Whenever this has happened I was surprised and gladdened because the patient was intensely interested in what could be seen outside, the changing weather, the clouds in the sky, the plants and flowers both in and outside the room. The patient was still so closely linked with 'the world' that he or she could become annoyed or cross. 'Just look, now that I can't tidy up this room any more, now someone else has to sort out my papers it's all so messy and untidy.' There is also the amusing irritation of the dying mother who, when her son comes into the room, says 'Couldn't you have cleaned your shoes better than that?' or 'The longer your hair gets the less you seem to comb it." or who shakes her head over the school report which is just as bad this term as last. So long as there is life there is not only hope but interest as well. Gradually this interest covers a smaller and smaller world, it flags more quickly, it grows more detached and disinterested. Still it keeps all the characteristics of the way in which this person lived his life. I believe that nothing illustrates more clearly that helping dying people is helping perfectly ordinary people.

7 Alternating between faith and doubt

The subject of faith itself is often raised. I said above that it is discussed as one of the elements of the personal life history. My impression is that alongside this, faith *per se* is also a subject for discussion. To be specific, I mean what we still believe to day, what the Christian Church still holds. Cecily Saunders[13] would like those who help the dying to do more than show concern for their immortal souls. Many patients want to *know* what community of faith there is in this world, what is it that all of us believe in these—secularised—times. This common belief has got to be mediated by the man or woman who is giving pastoral help. They will find themselves severely tested in this rôle. Do you believe anything yourself? What do you believe? The dying man sometimes sees his faith set against the background of the changing church, seeing himself as somebody who has been left out in the cold[14] or as someone who feels liberated, or who experienced a mixture of both feelings. But above all there is the longing —often expressed with real passion 'I want to believe, but what and how?' My impression is that many dying people are searching for the opportunity to purify their faith or to recover it, that they themselves want to 'theologise in the presence of death'.[15] Faith, it would seem, is becoming more and more wordless. It is taking on the perspective of the lover who goes out on a dark night in search of his beloved.[16] It is in this context that one can say that faith and death belong together.[17] For the deeper the faith becomes the more is there a consciousness of God, an intimacy with God which cannot be expressed in words. The dying person who has had the good fortune to have his faith grow into authentic religious faith, 'a divine virtue', can experience that 'death is his end but God is the end of death.'[18] This we cannot do all by ourselves: it must be mediated to us by someone else. That is why we want to know what 'they' believe, what 'the Church' believes today because it is in this actual period of history that we live and die.

In the next chapter I will discuss how faith contributes to ultimate self-realisation.

8 Longing for death

The last subject to be talked about is the longing for death. I have never met a dying person who did not begin to long for death. It can take different forms, some of them very moving. I shall always remember the patient who on the eve of Easter said to me 'Read me the Easter gospel now because I'm going to die tomorrow'. Next day he sank into an uninterrupted coma. On the other hand I have known an elderly woman who rapped impatiently on the sides of her bed, saying, 'This is all very well. I've lived quite long enough. The Lord should come and fetch me.' This after all is only an impatient way of saying 'Lord, now lettest thou thy servant depart in peace, according to thy word.'[19] 'I have seen everything by now, mine eyes have seen thy salvation.'[20] Now there's nothing to hold me back. This can be interpreted as an attempt to get one's own way, but in neither case was that my impression. These two people—and certainly these examples are not unique—felt that their lives had been fulfilled. Then the longing for death means: there has been enough suffering. I've done all I had to do. For my part, I don't ask for my life to be lengthened. Rather the reverse.

6

Becoming Oneself

WEISMAN[1] describes a dying woman who, the day after she had celebrated her birthday, became suddenly more alert and responsive than she had been for several weeks. She even put on make-up and for some inexplicable reason, held a rosary in her hands. She drew the doctor's attention to a painting of a bridge which had been hanging on the wall of her room ever since her admission into hospital. She was very curious, she said, to know what lay on the other side of the bridge which the picture did not reveal. The doctor tried to enter into her train of thought, praising her courage and adding that she was herself in process of crossing a kind of bridge. The rosary, he fancied, was a symbol of her thought about what lay before her. She said nothing in reply.

This doctor really listened to his patient. He saw her searching for the meaning of death and he understood what her present behaviour symbolised. Did he fully understand her? If he had grasped the full significance of these symbols, he might perhaps have said 'You are crossing a bridge; it is leading you to an unknown land but I see that you are not going alone. You are praying and you are also asking others to pray for you. With the rosary you are saying "Mother of God pray for us sinners now and at the hour of our death".'

In his actual reply the doctor was able to make contact with what the patient was thinking. But the second answer, I believe, would have resulted in a deeper contact. Why did the doctor draw back from this? Was he afraid because of his lack of pastoral competence? Did he not share the faith of his patient? Or was he ashamed to admit that he too was a believer?

It seems clear to me that the second answer accepts and strengthens the patient both in her search and in her faithful prayer. In this answer we try to accompany the patient, feeling where she is, moving at her pace, neither going ahead too fast, nor lagging behind. Seward Hiltner has formulated three principles of pastoral guidance. They are a) to sustain, b) to guide, c) to heal.[2]

The aim we can set ourselves depends on what is possible here and now with this particular patient. To sustain a dying person, to stay with him is always possible. It is still possible if the patient is hardly conscious. We can sit beside him, holding his hand if he can bear it. What we are giving is our faithful presence. But do we still want to guide this dying person? Where to? And do we also want to heal him? Heal him of what and why?

In this chapter I want to explain that the aim of pastoral counselling is to guide the patient to discover himself and to free him from self-alienation. Christian tradition leaves little doubt on this score. We want to lead the dying to their Lord who is himself the pastor, the shepherd. The poetic language of Psalm 23 expresses the purpose of this guidance quite accurately: the refreshment, the moving onward even in the darkness of death, the courage and the fulfilment of happiness and grace. It is to all this that we want to lead the dying. And therefore we offer our help to remove unhappiness, constraint and self-alienation. The goal of counselling is freedom, healing from 'sin' and guidance 'towards God', to whom the patient can say: 'Father, into thy hands I commit my spirit.'[3] 'It is accomplished.'[4]

The question now is whether we are able to translate this religious terminology into the language of ordinary human behaviour and whether by so doing we can learn how to die and to help others to die.

To some Christians this question will seem unnecessary and dangerous. They live in the conviction that religious words, the very Word of God, bring freedom and lead towards God. They fear that to introduce and to use psychological concepts, psychological 'translations', may turn pastoral counselling into some sort of half-baked social case-work or incompetent therapy, that psychology, pastoral psychology included, may blur the distinctions between these professional fields. On the other hand, there will also be those who say it is impossible to translate this religious language into practical objectives. The reason, they say, is that the language of Christian belief distracts man's attention from himself. J. Mathijsen puts this in a nutshell: 'To believe in the face of death seems to me like going to see a film when you have toothache.'[5] In other words, helping someone to believe is helping to distract him, helping to dull his pain, but not helping him to become himself.

This point of Mathijsen's had practical implications. It implies that Christian ministers can never offer pastoral guidance to dying unbelievers, humanists or those who lack a clearly defined faith. Or to put it another way, sensible modern people would do well, when dying, not to accept help from believers who will only distract them from the real issues of death. These are serious considerations.[6]

This makes me think of my first parish priest who during the last years of the war and the first year of liberation was asked on various occasions to help unbelievers in their hours of death or mourning. I have often thought about this. What did these people expect to get from him? They were all living along the River Zaan in a district where for many years church adherence has been at an abysmal level—as it is nearly everywhere now in Holland. They either had no religious upbringing of any sort or else their religious feelings had been badly, often irreparably damaged, through the Christian formation they had been given. This still remains true today. People have been damaged to such an extent that the old Christian terminology only evokes irritation or leaves them utterly indifferent. All the same, when confronted with the mystery of death, these same people want to reflect on who they are, how they have become what they are, what their life means, what they are on earth for. Maybe they have no wish to 'theologise in the face of death'[7] but they do want to philosophise and with many of them this search for wisdom is charged with a religious significance. They realise that wisdom is not in the wind, not in the fire, but in the still small voice.[8] They may have heard or felt that wisdom and enlightenment cannot be seized and held but are received by those who make themselves still and empty. Can Christian ministers help such people in their hours of death and mourning? They shouldn't think this is easy, but at the same time I believe, they must show their willingness to try. Often the question is no longer whether their Christian belief alienates people from themselves but whether they are able to make the promise of Christianity come true —that whoever loses his life for my sake will find it.[9] Can they help to make this true. Can Christians help people to find themselves? According to Mathijsen, their belief stands in the way. He compares it to a moving picture. Of course it is possible to forget your toothache or pain for a while in the cinema but the film itself does not take away toothache, much less death. Once out of the cinema you still have to take the appropriate measures. But then what is faith? Is it something like composing a gripping, diverting, or perhaps intensely dramatic story? The Bible certainly is full of human dramas, it is the product of human creativity, of the ability to dramatise human conflicts. It is shot through with the way in which human beings see 'Him who is invisible' at work.[10] Fortmann, whose major work bears these words of St Paul has paid serious attention to the question as to whether all these dramatic religious issues are not something more than the film we project. He has pointed out that the God to whom these believers surrender themselves, does not appear to them as a product of their own imagination. On the contrary, he reveals himself ever more as they dare to lose themselves. He calls them to 'the highest level of human existence' and says 'this would seem to be conditioned by man losing himself, not out of weakness . . . but in a conscious letting-go and self-emptying.'[11]

If Christians are to carry out the task to which their faith really calls them then they must be able to help people to give up their self-defence, to look into the self-revealing secret of life, without having to use the terminology of their own faith obtrusively. This calls for self-control but most of all, for a confidence rooted in their own faith. If Christians want to give pastoral help then they must be able to recognise in language that may be unfamiliar to them the intentions of God for these people. They must also be able to recognise the serious efforts made in Eastern thought to unmask and oppose our resistence against the unfamiliar, a resistance which continually blocks any possible encounter with 'the Other'.[12]

The question that now remains for Christians to ask is this —'Is the road towards ourselves also a road towards God?' I would like to discuss this more widely in the perspective of practical pastoral help. The question is exceedingly urgent for two reasons. First because more and more people reject the God they have been brought up to know—they reject him as an alien tyrant who jealously competes with them. They protest against him because he robs them of their 'self'. Christian ministers represent this tyrant. If this resistance is not worked through it can sometimes find dramatic expression just before death:

> 'I won't resist any longer.
> All I do is lie here and wait
> in case I am taken away tonight.
> Then the priest: I bring you the Lord.
> But with a final blow
> he flung away the cross from his lips
> screaming —Go away!
> Don't take away the last thing I possess!
> *My* sins go with me into *my* grave.'

This is how the Dutch poet H. M. Maarsman[13] describes this protest, this self-defence; no God outside myself.

At the same time a large number of people, among them leading figures in 'Humanistic Psychology' and 'Transpersonal Psychology' have set out to explore the unchartered areas of our human existence.[14] This interest in

inner experience has led, inevitably I would say, to an
interest in experiences of the transcendent. Here there is a
link with the work of Karlfried Graf Durckheim who for
many years has run a much-frequented centre for thera-
peutic meditation in Germany.[15] In 'Theologie en Pastorat'
and 'Ministerium' a gifted social worker tells what she
learned from Durckheim—to find her innermost self so that
she could listen to Christ in a way which until then she had
vainly searched for in her previous religious formation.
Now there should be no misunderstanding here. Pastoral
care of the dying does truly aim at helping a human being
to develop so that ultimately the desert of his inner life
blossoms, and he can experience the transcendent. This aim
is liable to two different misunderstandings: it may sound
elitist or it may sound unchristian. And yet I believe that
such misunderstanding can be removed by one single
example—that of the two men who were crucified with
Jesus.[16] Bible scholars vary in their interpretation of these
two men who were executed—whether they were rebels or
whether they were the equivalent of modern bank robbers.[17]
Be that as it may, I think we can only get an idea of this
terrible death by reading the reports of Amnesty Inter-
national about prisoners who have been tortured. And yet
in these circumstances one of these men experienced a
revelation. He recognised in this fellow sufferer Jesus, the
presence of 'the transcendent', and this enabled him to rise
above his sub-human situation to an understanding of a
community, of brotherhood and freedom: 'Lord, remember
me when you come into your kingdom.'

This story illustrates the certainty that this understanding,
this experience of the transcendent, is part of human poten-
tial. It is true of a man who was tortured to death, whose
pain received no alleviation and who nevertheless achieved
peace with himself. But it presupposed a meeting, an
encounter. Perhaps the question 'Is the way to oneself a way
towards God?' should be answered in this way: A pastoral
counselling which does not aim at helping the patient to

achieve peace with himself has no meaning. If it does bring such peace to people, the dying included, then conditions exist in which a person can understand the signs of God's presence, both within and outside himself. Whether in fact this will actually happen is something we have to wait for humbly.

7
Learning to support the dying

PASTORAL help for the dying is only secondarily a task for the professional clergy. It is first and foremost a task for all 'lay people'. Here I use the term 'lay people' in its twofold meaning.

Lay people are those who have not been trained in a particular skill. A non-medical man is a lay man. A non-clergyman is a lay man. But in the ecclesiastical sense of the word laymen, *laikou*, are those who belong to the *laos*, the People of God. It is to them that the mysteries of the kingdom have been entrusted and in this sense the lay people are equally the initiated. In the different Christian churches there is a varied division of tasks and responsibilities among lay people and clergy and this is subject to change. The changes have to do with the number of ministers available, with the laymen's wish to take responsibility, but above all, with the way in which people want to create a Christian community with one another. My belief that pastoral help for the dying, as I have described it, is primarily the laymen's job is based on the conviction that we are responsible for one another. And I am also convinced that unless this is so, the specific work of the clergy will come to nothing, will remain sterile.

The fact that I shall pay some attention in this chapter to the experiences of the minister or priest does not mean that care of the dying is their monopoly. But it does mean that their very ministry brings them extra problems, extra opportunities. For both groups, for clerics and laity it holds good that pastoral care for the dying must be learned.

Faber[1] has repeatedly said that the minister is considered to be 'a difficult person'. This springs from his work, his rôle and his personality. In the world of medicine which grows steadily more and more technological and where more trust

is put in facts and figures than in the handling of feelings
the minister represents things that are difficult and elusive.
On top of this he has to carry the burden of past history; the
experience of centuries makes one expect to meet a dicta-
torial and interfering man. The result is that doctors and the
majority of the nursing and technical staff harbour very
mixed feelings about him: he is old-fashioned, out of date,
at the best someone to be put up with. But he is certainly
not an equal and not a person to go out of your way for.

One could say with St Paul that he is 'the refuse of the
world, the offscouring of all (medical) things.'[2] On the other
hand, he is the representative of God and of our religious
experience and as such is a man who both holds us and
frightens us. Furthermore he reminds us of death and
according to reasonably reliable studies by Feifel[3] the choice
of a medical career is determined by 'an above average fear
of death.' The priest is a trial for the doctor, the doctor is a
trial for the priest. Each must blame himself for the situation.
Pruyser[4] particularly reproaches pries_ for their feelings of
inferiority with regard to doctors, especially to psychiatrists.
Whether this is true or not, it would be a good thing if both
ministers and doctors could each acquire more personal
confidence, become less defensive and more skilled in helping
the dying. It is my considered opinion that doctors have been
insufficiently trained to co-operate with other professionals.[5]
Kastenbaum and Aisenberg[6] point out however that the
priest's presence is also beneficial to the doctors and
nursing staff. Through his work, provided he does it
properly, he shows the staff that there is at least somebody
who still regards the dying patient as a person, an individual
worthy of the fullest attention. And because he helps the
patient to make a better response to his situation he also
makes it possible for the nursing staff in their turn to respond
better to the patient. P. Jansen[7] gives an instance of this,
describing a woman who had been a 'notorious' patient in a
number of general and psychiatric hospitals. She got this
reputation because she burdened her surroundings with

all the unresolved conflicts of her life. But at the end this difficult woman found peace with herself and with her God. When she received the sacrament of the sick it was a real celebration and quite a number of the nursing staff celebrated with her.

This example also illustrates that the pastoral relationship with dying patients brings the priest ever new challenges. Faber[8] is right in saying that helping the dying should be distinguished from psychotherapy. On the other hand communication with the dying is something one has to learn and I should like to add that in this field we can learn a great deal from psychotherapy. I hope that by now the minister's task has been sufficiently described in this book. Now let us consider it from the patient's angle. The patient wants to know what kind of man the priest is. He tries him out— is he true to his word, can he be counted on? Or is the priest himself afraid, is his concern genuine, is his faith the sort of faith that can move mountains?

Of course such a testing must affect the minister and he cannot come out of it unscathed. That does not matter provided that he never defends himself. 'It is the Lord who judges me'[9] and the judgement of God is full of compassion; he knows me better than I know myself. The basis of the priest's resilience and initiative must be his Christian confidence based on the experience of being a representative of Jesus. Van Kilsdonk[10] makes two observations that are relevant here. First, that a person with a living experience of the Bible grows into a judge of human nature, with an understanding of the deepest and loftiest human possibilities. Second, that pastoral help of this standard is certainly expected but very seldom offered. This last statement is only too true, often ministers themselves have to learn to open themselves to what Dürckheim calls 'the great experience.'[11] Of this, he says that it evokes a second innocence, makes us the children to whom Jesus promised the Kingdom and brings us infinitely closer to the things around us. Cecily Saunders has given a moving instance of this. 'I remember watching one man who could concentrate totally on the white hyacinth plant by his bed. I saw in him the relief of that moment of pure pleaure. Somehow it seemed to be saying to him: "The world to which you belong is good and can be trusted".[12] This is not a childishness that asks no questions, it means that a man has been through all the questions and avoided none of them. And what holds good for priests holds good for lay people too. They can only help the dying if they can look back to such experiences in themselves, if they have opened themselves to them and worked through them. This is how Oosterhuis expresses it:[13]

> When I was at a complete loss, less than myself
> and trembling with disillusionment, he spoke
> to me, putting the choice in front of me.
> 'Do you want to remain dead, or do you want
> to become alive?' He took me as he found me,
> he did not blame me for my past but he asked
> me 'Do you want it to be like this or do you
> want it to be different? Do you identify
> yourself with what is behind you—and then
> you are not fitted for the kingdom of God.
> Or do you identify yourself with the future?'
> 'But is there a future?' I asked. He answered
> 'Go with me'.

Notes

Chapter 1

1 Original title, *De dood heeft alle tijd*, Rya Luysterburg, Amsterdam 1972.
2 W. J. Berger, 'Pastoraat aan zieken thuis' in *Theologie en pastoraat* 1970, p.13.
3 Lindner Traugott, L. Lentner, A. Holl, *Priesterbild und Berufswahlmotive. Ergebnisse einer sozialpsychologische Untersuchung bei den Wiener Mittelschülern*, Wein 1963.
4 Donald C. Houts, 'Ministering to the Family Dimensions of Illness' in *Pastoral Psychology* 1967, n.11, pp. 36-44.
5 A. D. Weisman, *On Dying and Denying—A Psychiatric Study of Terminality*, New York 1972.
6 Peter Hofstede, *Tot onze diepe droefheid*, Baarn 1970, pp. 124-126.

Chapter 2

1 Thomas W. Klink, 'Preface to a Pastoral Theology of Ministry to the Dying' in *The New Shape of Pastoral Theology*, ed. William B. Oglesby Jr., Nashville and New York 1965, pp. 326-339.
2 Robert Fulton, *Death and Identity*, New York 1965, p. 102.
3 Paul W. Pruyser, 'The Use and Neglect of Pastoral Resources' in *Pastoral Psychology*, Sept. 1972, pp 5-17.
Paul W. Pruyser, 'The Master Hand, Psychological Notes on Pastoral Blessing' in *The New Shape of Pastoral Theology*, ed. William B. Oglesby Jr., Nashville and New York 1969, pp. 352-365.
4 R. Kastenbaum and Ruth Aisenberg. *The Psychology of Death*, New York 1972, p. 226.

Chapter 3

1 S. F. H. J. Berkelbach van der Sprenkel and F. J. M. Malmberg, *Wat geloven zij?* Amsterdam 1942.
2 James 2:19.
3 W. Zandbelt, 'Pastorale bijstand aan stervenden' in *Theologie en Pastoraat* 65 (1969) pp. 69-76.
J. van Laarhoven, 'De geschiedenis van de biechtvader' in *Tijdschrift voor theologie* 7 (1967) pp. 375 ff.
4 W. Zandbelt, *o.c.*

[5] A. Vergote, 'De geloofsdimensie in de toekomst' antropologische evaluatie in *Toekomst van de religie, religie van de toekomst* (report of the conference organised by the theological faculty in Nijmegen, March 1972), published by the editors of *Tijdschrift voor theologie*, pp. 83-100.

[6] A. van Dantzig, 'Psychologie van de doodsangst' in *De dood verandert*, edited in co-operation with the Humanist Society, Amsterdam (De Arbeiderspers) 1969, pp. 69-76.

[7] Preface of the Mass of the Dead: 'Vita mutatur, non tollitur'.

[8] Ps. 23:1.

[9] Ps. 31:6.

[10] Dies Irae: from the Mass for the Dead.
Liber scriptus proferetur
in quo totum continetur
unde mundus judicetur.

[11] A. van Dantzig, *o.c.*, p. 75.

[12] Gen. 37:9.

[13] H. Lips, 'De moderne mens en de dood' in *De dood verandert*, o.c., pp. 99-112.

[14] W. van Dooren, 'Denken over de dood' in *De dood verandert*, o.c., pp. 59-66.

[15] E. Schillebeeckx 'Leven ondanks de dood' in *Tijdschrift voor theologie* 10 (1970) n.4 and also in *Concilium*, 6 (1970) n.10.

[16] Cf. *The Roman Missal*, Vatican Edition 1970, for the various Masses and also the new prefaces for the dead.

[17] K. H. Misskotte, *Kennis en bevinding*, Haarlem 1969, p. 244.

[18] E. H. Erikson, *Identity*, *Youth and Crisis*, Faber and Faber London 1968 paperback 1971.

[19] R. Berkhof, 'De plaats van de dood in het christelijk geloof' in *De dood verandert*, o.c., pp. 29-36.

[20] Peter Hofstede, *Tot onze diepe droefheid*, Baarn 1970, pp. 135-139.

[21] H. C. Rümke, *Karakter en aanleg in verband met het ongeloof*, Amsterdam 1963.

Chapter 4

[1] Peter Hofstede, *Tot onze diepe droefheid*, Baarn 1970.

[2] Harrie Nouwen, in an unpublished thesis, to be found in

the Psychological Laboratory of the Catholic University of Nijmegen.

3 Lawrence Le Shan in: Margaretta K. Bowers a.o., De pastor aan het sterfbed (original title: Counselling the Dying), Nijmegen-Utrecht 1969 (series: Wegen tot Pastoraat).

4 Robert Kastenbaum and Ruth Aisenberg, The Psychology of Death, New York 1972, p. 218.

5 o.c., pp. 67-68.

6 Leonard Pearson, Death and Dying—Current Issues in the treatment of the dying person, Cleveland and London 1969. The anecdote is told in the preface.

7 R. W. Baer, A. Meyer, T. Moorman, A. Haats and D. de Vos, Verandering en hoop; Pastoraal-theologische verkeening van de dynamiek van de hoop in negen series pastorale gesprekken, Nijmegen 1970 (unpublished thesis, to be found in the Psychological Laboratory of the Catholic University of Nijmegen).

8 T. P. Hackett and A. D. Weisman, 'The Treatment of the Dying' in Journal of Pastoral Care, vol. XVIII (1964) n.2, p. 67.

9 Baer a.o., o.c., chapter 2, p. 26.

10 Mt. 19:6—one of the traditional Gospel readings in the Nuptial Mass.

11 I Thess. 4:13.

12 Mt. 18:20.

13 P. Jansen, Het bijstaan van de stervenden: Pastoraal-theologische reflectie op de bijstand aan stervenden door illustratie en nuancering vanuit een aantal gevalstudies. Nijmegen 1970 (unpublished thesis, to be found in the Psychological Laboratory of the Catholic University of Nijmegen).

14 H. A. Wegman, 'Liturgie met zieken en stervenden' in Tijdschrift voor liturgie 53 (1969) pp. 179-196.

Chapter 5

1 Elizabeth Kübler-Ross, On Death and Dying, Tavistock Publication 1970.

2 J. J. M. Michels and P. Sporken, De laatste levensfase, part 2 Medische stervenshulp, Bilthoven 1972.

3 Hella Haasse, Zelfportret als legkaart, Amsterdam 1954.

[4] H. C. I. Andriessen 'Groei en grens in de volwassenheid', Nijmegen-Utrecht, p. 358.

[5] P. Van der Klei's contribution to a symposium on dying with human dignity, held by the Faculty of Medicine, Nijmegen University, on the occasion of its anniversary celebration, 14 April 1973.

[6] O certe necessarium Adae peccatum,
quod Christi morte deletum est.
O Felix culpa,
quae talem ac tantem meruit habere Redemptorem.
Roman Missal from the 'Exultet' of the Easter Vigil.

[7] P. Sporken, *De laatste levensfase*, part 1: *Stevenshulp en euthenasie*, Bilthoven 1973.

[8] Mt. 11:28.

[9] R. W. Baer a.o., thesis *Verandering en Hoop*, Appendix I, p. 1.

[10] H. C. Rümke, *Karakter en aanleg in verband met het ongeloof*, Amsterdam 1963, p. 24.

[11] J. C. van Es, 'Ieder sterft zijn eigen dood', contribution to the symposium, Nijmegen 14 April 1973. (See note 5).

[12] C. van der Meer, 'De arts in confrontatie met de stervende', contribution to the symposium, Nijmegen 14 April 1973. (See note 5).

[13] Cecily Saunders, 'The Moment of Truth, Care of the Dying Person' in *Current Issues*.

[14] Godfried Bomans and Michel van der Plas, *In de kou*, Bilthoven 1973.

[15] J. Firet, 'Theologiseren ten overstaan van het einde' *Ministerium* p. 110. Semper Agenda, Apeldoorn.

[16] Works of St John of the Cross vol I translated and edited by E. Allison Peers, Burns Oates, London 1943. Stanzas 'wherein the soul sings of the happy chance which it had in passing through the dark night of faith, in detachment and purgation of itself, to union with the Beloved.
On a dark night, Kindled in love with yearnings—oh, happy chance!—
I went forth without being observed, My house being now at rest.
In darkness and secure, By the ladder, disguised: oh happy chance!—

In darkness and in concealment, My house being now at
rest.
In the happier night, In secret, when none saw me,
Nor I beheld aught, Without light or guide, save that
which burned in my heart.
This light guided me, More surely than the light of
noonday,
To the place where he (well I knew who!) was awaiting
me—
A place where none appeared.
Oh, night that guided me, Oh, night more lovely than
the dawn,
Oh, night that joined Beloved with lover,
Lover transformed in the Beloved!
Upon my flowery breast, Kept wholly for himself alone,
There he stayed sleeping, and I caressed him,
And the fanning of the cedars made a breeze.
The breeze blew from the turret As I parted his locks;
With his gentle hand he wounded my neck
And caused all my senses to be suspended.
I remained, lost in oblivion; My face I reclined on the
Beloved.
All ceased and I abandoned myself,
Leaving my cares forgotten among the lilies.'

[17] cf. Althans, quoted by Firet, *o.c.*, who expands this theme.
[18] J. Firet, *o.c.*
[19] Lk. 2:2:29.
[20] Lk. 2:30.

Chapter 6

[1] A. D. Weisman, *On Dying and Denying:* A Psychiatric
   Study of Terminality, New York 1972.
[2] Seward Hiltner, *Preface to Pastoral Theology*, New York
   1958.
[3] Lk. 23:46.
[4] John 19:30.
[5] J. A. M. Mathijsen in: Peter Hofstede, *Tot onze diepe
   droefheid*, Baarn 1970, p. 41.
[6] I have been wondering whether to pay so much attention
   to Mathijsen's statement. But then, the theory of so-
   called religious projection is nowhere so pithily expressed.

At the same time I believe that this statement shows all the woolly thinking with which a number of people, who in the past received a Dutch Catholic education, speak of the phenomenon of religion. Recently a friend of mine, a protestant minister, said he was annoyed and surprised to be constantly confronted with examples of such 'Catholic woolly thinking'.

[7] J. Firet, *o.c.*

[8] I Kings 19:11-13.

[9] Mt. 16:25.

[10] H. M. M. Fortmann, *Als ziende de Onzienlijke*, Hilversum 1968.

[11] H. M. M. Fortmann, Oosterse Renaissance, Bilthoven 1972, pp. 59-60.

[12] *Yoga en Vedanta*, p. 15 (1973); 'There is no road from red to blue', pp. 24 ff.

[13] H. M. Marsman, 'Verset' in *Verzamelde gedichten*, Amsterdam 1941.

[14] J. M. van der Lans, 'Humanistic Psychology en vorming' in *Netherlands- Belgisch tijdschrift voor edukatief werk*, 22 (1973) 4, pp. 67 ff.

[15] Karlfried Graf Dürckheim, Durchbruch zum Wesen, Zürich 1954; 'Auf dem Wege zur Transparanz' in Günther Schulz (ed.), *Transparante Welt; Festschrift zum sechzigsten Geburstag van Jean Gebser*, Bern-Stuttgart, pp. 228-255.

[16] Lk. 23:42.

[17] B. Alfrink, *Het passieverhaal der vier evangelisten*, Utrecht-Nijmegen 1946, p. 151.

Chapter 7

[1] H. Faber, 'Pastorale begeleiding van stervenden' in *Over dood en sterven*, Leiden 1971, pp. 84-95.

[2] I Cor. 4:13.

[3] R. Kastenbaum and R. Aisenberg, *The Psychology of Death*, pp. 215-216 (Feifel's inquiry).

[4] Paul W. Pruyser, 'The Use and Neglect of Pastoral Resourses' in *Pastoral Psychology*, September 1972, pp. 5-17.

[5] The quotation is from Dr Karl Menninger. In my book *Op weg naar empirische zielzorg* I have described a

situation in which Karl Menninger brings this home to
his students in a very drastic way.

6 R. Kastenbaum and R. Aisenberg, o.c.

7 P. Jansen, *Het bijstaan van stervenden; Pastoraal-
theologische reflectie op de bijstand aan stervenden, door
illustratie en nuancering vanuit een aantal gevalstudies.*
Unpublished thesis, Nijmegen 1970, to be found in the
Psychological Laboratory of the Catholic University,
Nijmegen.

8 H. Faber.

9 I Cor. 4:4.

10 J. van Kilsdonk, 'Pastor en psychiater in crisis' in
Maandblad voor Geestelijke Volksgezondheid 4 (1973)
pp. 181 ff.

11 What I am describing here is a state of mind described by
three scholars. Graf Dürckheim, Fortmann and Vergote
from three different viewpoints. Dürckheim came to this
through the way of Zen Buddhism, Fortmann through
the study of primitive cultures and Vergote through study
of the structures of the child's relationship to the world.
Each of them is saying in different words that after all our
critical studies, we have to regain the simplicity and
richness of a non-aggressive, open-minded, childlike
relation to the world. T. S. Eliot says something of this in
his *Four Quartets;*

'We shall not cease from exploration
And the end of all our exploring
Will be to arrive at where we started
And to know the place for the first time.'

This is a particular problem for those who have to go
through the process of de-mythologising and then find
that myth and symbols are the only way in which we can
feel at home with the mysteries of life and the universe.
This second 'primitiveness' is the result of an inner
development in which we re-integrate thinking and the
deep sources of our religious feelings.
See Karlfried Graf Dürckheim, *Im Zeichen der grossen
Erfahrung*, Munich-Planegg 1951. See also H. M. M.
Fortmann, *Als ziende de Onzienlijke II*, p. 248 and IIIb,
p. 78 where he speaks about the second primitiveness.

See also A. Vergote in *De Onbevangenheid* (brochure 2-2, second series, Geestelijke Volksgezondheid), Bilthoven 1973.

[12] Cecily Saunders *o.c.* p. 76.

[13] Huub Oosterhuis, *Zien-soms even*. Bilthoven 1972, p. 90.

ADDITIONAL READING LIST

AUTTON, Norman. *From Fear to Faith: Studies of Suffering and Wholeness.* 1971 S.P.C.K. £0·90 paperback.

AUTTON, Norman. *Pastoral Care of the Dying.* Library of Pastoral Care. 1966 S.P.C.K. £1·00 paperback.

BOROS, Ladislas. *Moment of Truth: Mysterium Mortis.* 1972 Search Press £1·50 paperback.

ELBERT, Edmund. *I Understand.* Sheed and Ward 1973 £3·50.

FABER, Heije. *Pastoral Care in the Modern Hospital.* 1971 S.C.M. Press £2·00.

HINTON, John. *Dying.* 1972 (r.e.) Penguin Books, £0·40 paperback.

LACK, Sylvia and Lamerton, Richard. ed. *The Hour of Our Death.* 1974 Geoffrey Chapman. £1·65.

LAMERTON, Richard. *Care of the Dying.* Priory 1973 £2·50.

SHOTTER, E. F. ed. *Matters of Life and Death.* 1964 Darton, Longman and Todd. £0·75 paperback.

STEPHENS, Simon. *Death Comes Home.* 1972 Mowbrary £0·60 paperback.

Care of the Dying: a Symposium. 1972 H.M.S.O. £0·65.

Some Grail Publications

THE CHURCH AND COMMUNITY DEVELOPMENT

A short incisive book by George Lovell, a Methodist minister with ten years experience in community development work. He takes as his starting point that all Christians and all local churches have, as part of their mission, to create and sustain community. Illustrated.   75p plus postage.

THIS IS THE CHURCH

Republished by popular demand. A Grail simplification of Lumen Gentium, the most vital of all the decrees to have emanated from the Second Vatican Council.   30p plus postage.

DISCUSSION PROMPTERS

Discussion material for groups, who are invited to explore a wide range of experiences, points of view, attitudes, problems and action. The book is divided into ten sections and each section provides material for three meetings.   30p plus postage.

SPARKS FLY UPWARD

Material for discussion but this time expressly geared for religious communities, both of men and women. Each 'situation' is linked with a passage from Scripture. The purpose of this is to introduce a new dimension or to open up some aspect of the situation being considered by the group.   35p plus postage.

THINK CARDS

Cards which appeal to people of different religious affiliations and also to people who reject recognised religious structures.

First Series GR 1–12

Quotations from Christian, Jewish, Hindu and Muslim writings are presented with bold and free calligraphic design. Two or three colours.   *continued*

Second Series GR 15–24

Cards which incorporate photography and quotations from varied sources. Two or three colours.

In both series there are cards intended for joyful occasions and cards that strike a positive and consoling note in times of bereavement or sorrow.   Per card 3p plus postage.
Discount on 150 cards, 10 per cent.
Size 3 ins. x 5 ins.